W9-CDJ-371

INTRODUCTION

Stenciling is one of the earliest forms of interior decoration found in the newly formed United States of America. While stenciling was generally known to the world of that time, the subject matter and work methods that developed in the new nation were distinctly early American. The period in which early American stenciling was popular lasted nearly a hundred years, from 1775 to around 1860. Walls, floors, furniture and fabrics adorned with the simple or ornate patterns of that era have been saved in museums and private collections across the country. Authentic early American stencilwork has been found only as far west as Ohio. Stenciling was forgotten for a while when the Industrial Revolution made assembly-line wallpapers and woven goods available to the majority of the people.

The subjects chosen as stencil designs reflect the life of the early American settlers: patriotic American eagles, native flowers, leaves, acorns and running vines. The pineapple, symbol of hospitality, was a favorite. Classical motifs were popular, and romantic hearts and weeping willow trees bespoke the uncomplicated nature of the early settlers. Baskets and urns filled with flowers and fruits expressed the abundance and plenty in early America.

Once stenciling was introduced in America there was no object that might not be adorned with the graceful patterns. Walls were handsomely decorated along with wood floors and canvas floorcloths. Furniture of every description including chairs, chests, picture frames, bedboards, tables, window cornices and boxes of all shapes and sizes came under the hand of the itinerant stenciler. Tinware, then known as tole, was handsomely decorated with gold powders. Canisters, coffeepots, tin lampshades and boxes were stenciled in simple designs. Rectangular metal trays of the era were stenciled with intricate borders and ornate central designs. The resourceful women of early America adapted stenciling for decorating bedspreads, pillow covers, curtains, window shades and tablecloths for special occasions.

This book is filled with authentic early American stencil designs that can be cut out and used for decorating walls, floors, furniture, fabrics, tin, leather and almost any other surface. All materials needed are inexpensive and easy to find in most well-stocked hardware or art-supply stores. The method is easily mastered and projects quickly completed.

LIST OF MATERIALS

boiled linseed oil	masking tape
turpentine	paint
rags	textile paint (for fabric)
stencil knife and blades	stenciling brushes
knife sharpener or carborundum stone	newspaper
	fine sandpaper
large knitting needles or ice pick	desk blotters (for fabric)
cutting surface (glass, wood, etc.)	varnish (for floors, wood, tin)

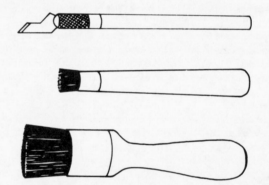

Stencil knife and two stenciling brushes of different sizes.

First, cut out an entire page (= stencil plate) from the book with a pair of scissors. When more than one design appears on a page, a dotted line serves as the cutting guideline for separating each design onto a distinct stencil plate. The margin of ¾ inch or more around the design makes the stencil sturdy and durable while in use and protects the surrounding areas from paint when stenciling.

The pages of this book are of medium-weight manila paper, which must be treated with oil to make it tough, leathery and impervious to moisture. Oiled manila will become semi-translucent, allowing light to penetrate slightly. A knife blade will cut through an oiled plate more easily. The oiling process takes place after the plate (page) is cut from the book but before the blacked-in areas of the design are cut out, so there will be no chance of bending or ripping delicate ties (bridge areas) when applying the oil.

A mixture of 50% *boiled* linseed oil and 50% turpentine is applied with a rag to both sides of the plate until it is thoroughly saturated. Using a thumbtack, the plate is then hung to dry. It will dry to the touch in about 10 minutes. Any excess can be wiped off with a dry rag or the plate can be allowed to dry for a longer period. The rag should then be immersed in water until it can be incinerated or removed by regular garbage disposal service. Spontaneous combustion can occur if the rag is stored for later use.

The stencil knife is used for cutting out the small pieces through which the paint will reach the surface to be decorated. Only the solid black areas of each design are cut out. Suitable cutting surfaces for this task are hard wood, a piece of plate glass with the edges taped, or a stack of old newspapers. The oiled stencil plate is placed on the cutting surface and allowed to move freely. Grasp the stencil knife as you would a pencil. Apply even pressure for the entire length of a curve or line. Frequent lifting of the knife causes jagged, uneven edges. The small details of the stencil design are cut out first and larger areas last to prevent weakening the plate before cutting is completed. Sharpen the blade frequently on a carborundum stone or knife sharpener.

Cutting requires careful and accurate work. A jagged line or ragged corner will stencil exactly that way in every impression of the stencil plate.

The narrow bridges of paper between the cut-out areas in the design are known as ties. If you accidentally cut through a tie, apply tape to both sides of the tear and replace the tape when needed. Circles and small dots are difficult to cut with a knife. Various large needles can be used to punch out the circles. Ice picks and different-size knitting needles work well. Carefully use the knife or a small piece of fine sandpaper to trim and smooth the edges.

Paints used for stenciling can be water-base or turpentine-base. Any paint used must be mixed to a fairly thick consistency. Acrylic paint is an excellent water-base paint because it is fast-drying and easy to clean up. Acrylics are sold in tubes or jars and come in the right consistency for stenciling. Japan paints come in small 8-oz. cans and must be thinned slightly with turpentine. Turpentine-base paints must be allowed to dry for 24 hours. Both acrylic and japan paint dry to a flat finish. As soon as stenciling is completed, brushes are cleaned, using water for water-base paints and turpentine for oil or turpentine-base paints.

Stenciling on fabrics requires textile paints or inks made especially for decorating on fabric. Textile paints and inks come either water- or turpentine-soluble and are mixed thinner than regular paints. The fabric must be prewashed or drycleaned to remove any sizing and allow for shrinkage. Blotters must be used underneath the fabric to absorb excess moisture and paint. After the stenciled fabric has dried, ironing will set the textile paint or ink and make the colors permanent and washable. All these coloring mediums can be purchased at an art-supply store.

Brushes used for stenciling are cylindrical. The bristles are cut all the same length, forming a circular flat surface of bristle ends. Stencil brushes come in various sizes. A good selection of sizes would be ¼ inch in diameter, ½ inch in diameter, and 1 inch in diameter.

A clean brush is used each time a new color is introduced.

Stenciling begins by securing the stencil plate on two sides with masking tape to the object being stenciled. If the plate is not secure, the action of the stencil brush will cause the design to smear. The brush is grasped like a pencil but held perpendicular to the work surface. Dip only the flat bottom of the bristles into the paint. Do not overload the brush with paint, or it will run under the plate and ruin the design. Have several sheets of newspaper nearby for pouncing out the freshly loaded brush. Pouncing is a hammerlike movement that disperses the paint throughout the bristles. When an even speckling of paint is evident on the newspaper, the brush is ready for use. Stippling is the proper term for the rapid up-and-down motion of the brush over the stencil plate. Stippling continues until the openings in the plate are completely filled in with color.

Several plates in this book have two parts for stenciling in more than one color. The A-plate is stenciled first, and when the paint is dry the B-plate is transferred over the matching parts of the A-stencil. Remember that only the solid black areas of the B-plate design are cut out. Small details from the A-plate design will show when the B-plate is superimposed. These details will enable the stenciler to line up the B-plate correctly.

Masking tape is used to keep different colors clean and separate if you desire to use more than one color for a single stencil plate. The varying parts of the design are masked with tape as each color is transferred. Changing the masking tape is done without removing the plate from the project being stenciled.

The border designs in this book run continuously. On the right or left side of the stencil plate is a portion of the design that is repeated exactly on the opposite side. With each new setting, the design is lined up over its matching place in the previous impression. In this manner the border can run to any length neatly and in a straight line.

As soon as stenciling with any plate is finished, the plate is wiped gently with a rag or sponge dampened with water or turpentine depending on the paint in use. This increases the life expectancy of the stencil plate by helping prevent the accumulation of paint around the edges of the design.

Certain colors are distinctly early American. Vegetable juices, earth minerals and soot limited the range of hues that early stencilers employed. Bright vermilion to dull brown-red, bright yellow to ochre, Prussian blue, light blue-grey, medium grey-green, dull green and the earth browns completed the early American palette. The cover illustrations will give a good idea of the color range.

When mixing colors for stenciling, the addition of raw umber will grey any color and simulate the appearance of age. Sanding the stenciled design with fine sandpaper will make it appear worn. Stencilwork on floors, woodwork, and tin should be protected with several coats of a good varnish.

A more detailed and specific account of the art of stenciling is contained in *The Complete Book of Stencilcraft* (Simon & Schuster), by the author of this book.

1A

Cut out black areas only.

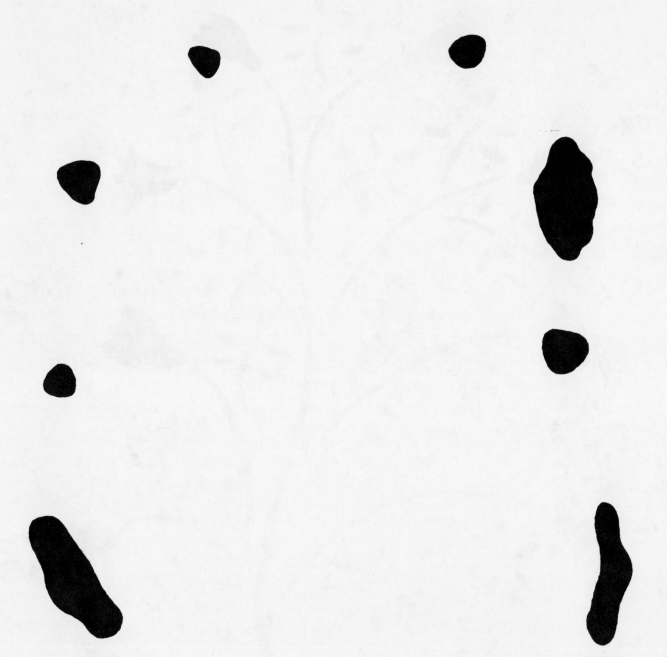

Cut out black areas only.

2B

3A

Cut out black areas only.

4

7

8

9

Cut out black areas only.

10A

10B

14

15

16

18

19

20

21

25

26

27

28

29

30

33

34

35

36

37

38

39

40

41

42

43

44

45

46

47

48

49

50

53A

53B

Cut out black areas only.

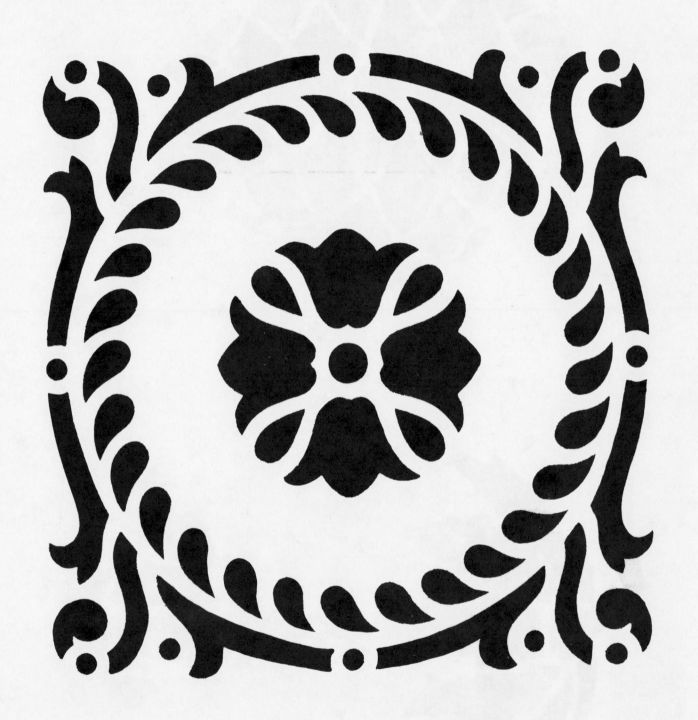